Exploring Earth's Resources

Using Plants

Sharon Katz Cooper

Heinemann Library
Chicago, Illinois

Customer Service   888–363–4266

Visit our website at www.heinemannraintree.com

Designed by Michelle Lisseter
Printed and bound in China, by South China Printing Company

11 10 09 08 07
10 9 8 7 6 5 4 3 2 1

Library of Congress Cataloging-in-Publication Data

Katz Cooper, Sharon.
   Using plants / Sharon Katz Cooper.
       p. cm. -- (Exploring Earth's resources)
   Includes index.
   ISBN-13: 978-1-4034-9316-3 (library binding - hardcover)
   ISBN-10: 1-4034-9316-2 (library binding - hardcover)
   ISBN-13: 978-1-4034-9324-8 (pbk.)
   ISBN-10: 1-4034-9324-3 (pbk.)
 1. Plants--Juvenile literature. I. Title.
   QK49.K18 2007
   581.6'3--dc22

                                                    2006029709

Acknowledgments
The publishers would like to thank the following for permission to reproduce photographs:
Action Plus p. **17** (Glyn Kirk); Alamy pp. **14** (Visions of America, LLC), **15** (Tom Tracy Photography); Anthony Blake Photo Library p. **13**; Corbis pp. **5** (Matt Brown), **7** (Louie Psihovos), **8** (Zefa/Theo Allofs), **12**, **13** (Nik Wheeler), **17**, **18** (Walter Hodges); Eye Ubiquitous p. **16**; GeoScience Features Picture Library p. **9**; Getty Images pp. **4** (Jan Tove Johansson), **21** (Stone/John Humble); Harcourt Education LTD p. **22** (Tudor Photography); Masterfile pp. **11** (Peter Christopher), **20** (Lloyd Sutton); Photolibrary pp. **6** (Frithjof Skibbe), **10** (Botanica); Science Photo Library pp. **17** bottom left (Pat & Tom Leeson), **17** bottom right (Will & Deni Mcintyre); Science Photo Library p. **19** (Philippe Psaila).

Cover photograph reproduced with permission of Corbis.

Contents

Some words are shown in bold, **like this**.
You can find them in the glossary on page 23.

What Are Plants?

Plants are living things.

They use sunlight to make their own food.

Plants are **natural resources**.

Natural resources come
from Earth.

Do All Plants Look the Same?

There are many different types of plant.

Some plants have colorful flowers.

Some plants grow quickly and some grow slowly.

Some plants are tiny, like violets. Some plants are huge, like trees.

Most plants grow on land.

Some plants live in shallow water.

There are plants that grow on other plants.

What Do Plants Need to Grow?

All plants need water and light.

Some plants need a lot of sun.
Others grow best in the shade.

Most plants need soil to grow in.

All plants need **carbon dioxide** from the air.

How Do We Use Plants?

We eat some plants.

Farmers grow many different fruits and vegetables.

cinnamon

Spices come from plants.

We use spices in cooking. This spice is cinnamon.

We use plants to make furniture and build houses.

Workers cut down trees to make them into planks of wood.

paper

We use wood from trees to make paper.

We use wood from trees as fuel, too.

Many people burn wood to make fires for heat and cooking.

Cotton comes from a plant.
We use cotton to make clothes.

We also use plants to make
many **medicines**.

17

Who Studies Plants?

Foresters are scientists who study forests.

They decide which trees we can cut down without running out.

Other plant scientists help farmers grow healthy crops.

Will We Ever Run Out of Plants?

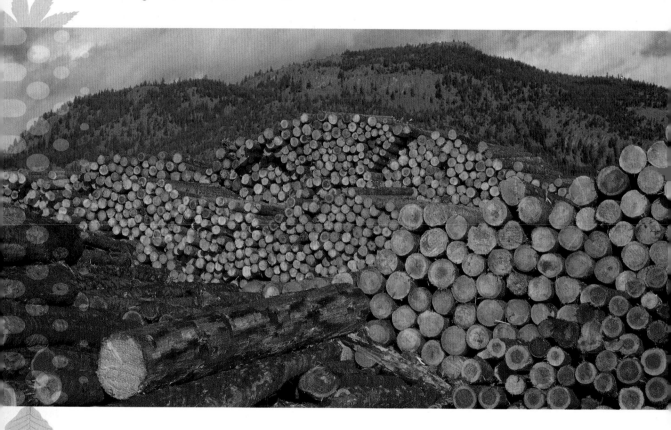

Plants usually grow back. They are **renewable**.

But if we use plants too quickly, we may run out before they can grow back.

To use plants more slowly, we can **recycle** paper.

We can find new uses for old wood.

Plants Quiz

Take a look around your house or classroom. Can you find ten things that are made from plants?

Glossary

 **carbon dioxide** gas that plants need to breathe

 **forester** scientist who studies forests

 **medicine** something that helps people get better if they are sick

 **natural resource** material from Earth that we can use

 **recycle** reuse something that has already been used

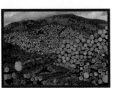 **renewable** something that will not run out

Index